The Naughty Mussel Recipes Book

Keith Pepperell

ISBN-13: 978-1985573109

ISBN-10: 1985573105

DEDICATION

To my spawn Jack, Lydia, and Alex none of whom are fold of mussels or vacuum cleaning

ACKNOWLEDGMENTS

Lady Joan Pepperell

Sir Francis Pepperell

Trevor Lang

Stephen Knapper

Lady Estima Davenport

Lady Ophelia Merkin

Sir Quimbus Merkin

Muriel Dinwiddy

Davin Monniaux — Image

Zytheme — Image

Bundesarchiv — Image

Consell Comarcal del Baix Empordà - Image

1 THE NAUGHTY MUSSEL

For all of you plucky linguists and

wordsmiths the word 'mussel' derives from

the "Old English muscle, musscel "shellfish,

mussel," from Late Latin muscula (source of

Old French musle, Modern French moule,

Keith Pepperell with Lady Estima Davenport

Middle Dutch mosscele, Dutch mossel, Old High German muscula, German Muschel), from Latin musculus "mussel," literally "little mouse," also "muscle;" like muscle, derived from mus "mouse" on the perceived similarity of size and shape.

The modern spelling, distinguishing the word from muscle, first recorded c. 1600, not fully established until 1870s.''

The naughty French call these tasty little beasts 'moules'.The surname Mussel seems to have been first recorded in the Fen District of Lincolnshire, England in about 1200. It is likely derived from a common occupation there, that of mussel gatherer. There are other variations of the surname that include Musel, Mussell, Muscel, Muswel, Muscelle and many others.

That high and late Middle Ages scribbler Geoffrey Chaucer writes in The Summoner's Tale, "and **Mussel** Quod he, "for many a muscle and many an oystre, Mussels oistres

and muscles and oothir swich Must He moste

preche, and wel affile his tonge . And telle he

moste his tale, as was resoun, We moste

endure: this is the short and playn." For

whom that I mostenedes lese my lyf. As

forward was..."

We find a mussel reference in Shakespeare's

Merry Wives of Windsor {IV, 5} when

naughty Falstaff says "Ay marry, was it,

mussel-shell what would you do with her?"

We can also find very modern examples of

mussel poetry as in Brian Strand's 2009

masterpiece *Finger Fork Buffet*

"A polato frittata

Three cheese lasagne

Saffron and mussel tartlets

An iced-lime cheesecake

or

Goats' cheese souffle

Chardonnay

Light !"

Also there is always Gry Christensen's deeply

moving 2014 work *The Anchor*

"I once loved

an anchor

one of those

that sails

on skin

Keith Pepperell with Lady Estima Davenport

one of those

that has

a rowing heart

and pelting blood

within
One of those
who blows
mussel covered
kisses
one of those
that tells
mermaids salty lies
one of those
who'll
go down with
rum and shackles
the day he finally
dies."

Also, we must not forget Frances Schiavina's

alluring 2017 work *Ode to a Mussell* (sic)

A palace on the rocks

washed by the sea

impregnable and strong

fit for a queen

softened by a carpet

of Ulva green

dotted with coins

of Halimeda weed

adorned with peacocks

fan Padina

and feathery Caulerpa

red, pink, and green

lulled by the waves

fed by the sea

fit for the beauty

of a mussel queen.

And certainly not Ilene Bauer's 2015 delight

At The Mussel Restaurant which also makes

the author copiously drool with moist

anticipation when she writes,

At the mussel restaurant
You order up a pot.
Ceremoniously, they're served,
Piled high and piping hot.
Scoop some shells and use your tiny
Fork to pull the meat.
Sop the sauce with crusty bread,
Each bite a tasty treat.
Sip a draft beer and relax
For everything's all right.

The Naughty Mussel Recipes Book

A mussel feast's the perfect way
To welcome Friday night.

Poet Gary Smith's haunting 2016 poem Oh
to be a Fish enigmatically reveals the salty
yearnings of a poor mussel when he writes,

I'm clinging to a rock,
Being battered by the waves.
At the mercy of the sea,
Living long and tedious days.
No escape for me,
Life's a constant tussle
Relentlessly being pounded,
It's not easy being a mussel.
Stuck here on this rock
Filtering away all day.
Nothing to eat but plankton,

Keith Pepperell with Lady Estima Davenport

I wish I could swim away.

Oh, to be a fish

And cruise the open sea,

I may be shackled to my rock,

But I dream of being free.

And finally here, we must never forget

Jackie Chou's 2016 masterwork I am Sushi,

I am your clam, your mussel

I am your tuna, your salmon

I am your cream cheese

I am your rice, white and full-figured

I am your peculiar cilantro

I am your wasabi

I am your sweet ginger

Am I a delicacy?

Do I taste good?

Don't you think you had too much meat?

Maybe I should have more carrot and more

cucumber.

But still, I am sushi

That's what's important to me

I wish I could be more enthusiastic about

mussel poetry but sadly I remain particularly

unmoved.

I am however very fond of many artworks

that include mussel imagery.

In particular, the naughty Dutch seem to do

a fine job of a delightful tongue-in-shell use

of the alluring bivalve.

Often they use the mussel shell as a vessel to

satirically transport groups of Dutch rascals.

Keith Pepperell with Lady Estima Davenport

Some quite decent examples of this follows.

CONCHA PROCELLOSVM DIC QVA SPE NAVIGAT AEQVOR·

13

Johann Theodor de Bry 1596

The Mussel Shell

Hieronimus Bosch
Garden of Earthy Delights c. 1480

Pieter van der Heyden – Pretmakers in
een mossel op zee (1562)

Mussels – 1876

For my naughty biologist chums 'Mussel' is the common name for several families of bivalve mollusks that live in both freshwater and saltwater. They are a naughty edible clams (not the bearded clam) having an elongated and asymmetrical common shell. We most often use the term 'mussel' to describe the naughty edible bivalves.

The word "mussel" is most frequently used to mean the naughty edible bivalves of the marine family Mytilidae residing happily along the exposed shores of intertidal zones. They attach themselves by their naughty beards (hence 'bearded clam') or byssal threads to firm substrates (rocks, sea-wrecks or in commercial fishing ropes of various kinds.

"In most marine mussels the shell is longer than it is wide, being wedge-shaped or asymmetrical. The external colour of the shell is often dark blue, blackish, or brown, while the interior is silvery"

Freshwater mussel species inhabit lakes, ponds, rivers, creeks, canals, and they are classified in a different subclass of naughty of bivalves.

Annoying freshwater zebra mussels are not

related to the former groups and are more

often associated with other species of clams.

'The mussel's external shell is composed of

two hinged halves or "valves". The valves are

joined together on the outside by a ligament,

and are closed when necessary by strong

internal muscles (anterior and posterior

adductor muscles). Mussel shells carry out a

variety of functions, including support for

soft tissues, protection from predators and

protection against desiccation."

Further it is noted "Like most bivalves,

mussels have a large organ called a foot. In

freshwater mussels, the foot is large, muscular, and generally hatchet-shaped. It is used to pull the animal through the substrate (typically sand, gravel, or silt) in which it lies partially buried. It does this by repeatedly advancing the foot through the substrate, expanding the end so it serves as an anchor, and then pulling the rest of the animal with its shell forward. It also serves as a fleshy anchor when the animal is stationary."

As we shall see *post* the naughty beard is removed prior to preparating for eating or better 'gobbling down'.

Mussels are filter feeders and like nothing better than a big 'ol mess of plankton orother microscopic sea creatures which are free-floating in seawater. "A mussel draws water in the ciliaon the gils for all-you-can-eat ciliary-mucus feeding. The wastewater exits through the excurrent siphon. The labial palps finally funnel the food into the mouth, where digestion begins. Mussels can be found clumping together in mussel gangs often on wave-washed rocks, each attached to the rock by its byssus. For mussels the buffet is almost always open except perhaps at low tide when some naughtily expose themselves.

Mussels have quite dull sex lives.

They areeated by humans, republicans, the French, seabirds, starfish, whelks, otters, racoons, ducks, and geese. Gangs of punk starfish consume the most it seems.

The naughty Chinese consume most mussels in the global market (about 40%). Europeans have cultivated them for thousands of years and they are particularly beloved by the Spanish and the French.

Most commercially produced (cultured) mussels in North America come from Prince Edward Island and Newfoundland with a growing Washington State industry.

Uncultured mussels slurp down their plankton and have unkemp byssus.They also trash talk other clams and try to grab the bearded ones.

Our ancestors often used mussel shells to compete ablutions particularly in coastal regions prior to toilet paper's popularity (approx. 1900). {See Pepperell K., *Sponging, Scraping, and Wiping in the Garderobes of Medieval English Castles*, Ohio Medieval Colloquium (2010)}.

2. EATING MUSSELS

Keith Pepperell with Lady Estima Davenport

Humans have used the 17 species of edible mussels as food for thousands of years. Freshwater mussels are generally considered to be nastily unpalatable even by republicans and the French (who will eat almost anything). Oddly and historically the native North American peoples ate them widely

Some Europeans enjoy them with fries (moules-frites) particularly in Belgium, Netherlands, and France,. The author's favorites are the large, plump, succulent, naughty Asian green mussels that most often farmed in verdant New Zealand and are enjoyed in Thai cuisine.

Mussels are versatile little buggers as some of the recipes *post* will clearly attest.

Herbs, shallots, garlic, butter, lemon, and white wine are common ingredients in some delightful preparations.

Mussels can be baked, steamed (most common), boiled, or served as as 'tigres' — mixed with other seafood including fish and shrimp and then quickly fried and served in the empty and well-cleaned half shell.

Mussels can also be picked or smoked with the latter being an inexpensive favorite

While living in Turkey I enjoyed them flour covered and then fried accompanied by many buckets of Efes Pilsen beer.

As is talso the case with cockles, minkles, and whelks vinegar is an excellent seasoning and I have enjoyed them freshly boiled in a light vinegar in Ireland.

I get the naughty plump green mussels at my local Chinese restaurant (Cantonese specialities) cooked in a delightful garlic and fermented black bean broth.

Humans have used the 17 species of edible mussels as food for thousands of years.

Freshwater mussels are generally considered to be unpalatable even by republicans and the French (who will eat almost anything) , though historically the native North American peoples ate them widely.

Some Europeans enjoy them with fries (moules-frites) particularly in Belgium, Netherlands, and France,. The author's favorites are the large, plump, succulent, naughty Asian green mussels that most often farmed in verdant New Zealand and are widely enjoyed in naughty Thai cuisine.

They were commonly eaten as a street food

Keith Pepperell with Lady Estima Davenport

in England and the well-known song

featuring the always naughty Molly Malone

will attest. There is an attractive statue to

the redoubtable lady in Dublin's fair city.

Sweet Molly Malone's Alluring Bronze
Statue in Dublin, Eire

You will doubtless recall the popular old

ditty,

In Dublin's fair city,

Keith Pepperell with Lady Estima Davenport

Where the girls are so pretty,

I first set my eyes on sweet Molly
Malone,

As she wheeled her wheel-barrow,

Through streets broad and narrow,

Crying, "Cockles and Mussels, alive, alive,
oh!"

"Alive, alive, oh,

Alive, alive, oh,"

*Crying "Cockles and mussels, alive, alive,
oh".*

She was a fishmonger,

But sure 'twas no wonder,

For so were her father and mother

before,

And they wheeled their barrows,

Through the streets broad and narrow,

Crying, "Cockles and mussels, alive, alive, oh!"

(chorus)

She died of a fever,

And no one could save her,

And that was the end of sweet Molly Malone.

But her ghost wheels her barrow,

Through streets broad and narrow,

Crying, "Cockles and mussels, alive, alive, oh!"

Cultured Rope Mussels

BULL. U. S. B. F., 1910.   PLATE XVII.

FIG. 68.

Mussel Dredging

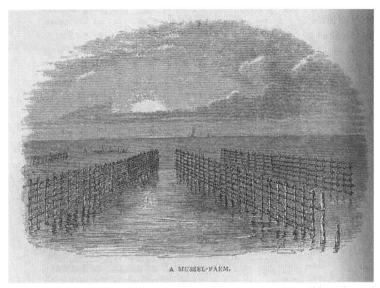

A MUSSEL-FARM.

A Mussel Farm

Swarthy Mussel People in Iowa

Keith Pepperell with Lady Estima Davenport

Cooking Mussels on the Mississippi

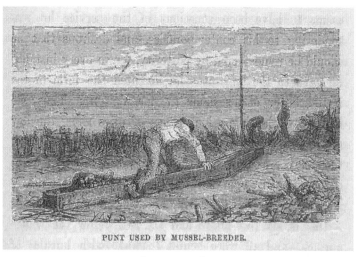

PUNT USED BY MUSSEL-BREEDER.

A Mussel Breeder's Punt

Mussel Collecting Through the Ice

A Naughty Bar and Crowfoot Outfit for Taking Mussels, Consisting of John Boat, Two Bars with Crowfoot Hooks, and the 'Mule' (Lying on Stern of Boat) 1921

3. THE RECIPES

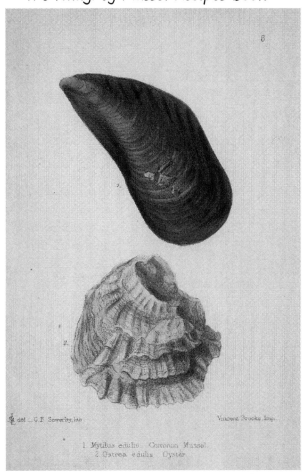

A Common Naughty Mussel (Mytilis Eclulis) and its Special Friend the Delightful Naughty Oyster (Ostrea Edulis) in 1883

1. Apicius Naughty Roman Mussels from De re Coquinaria

The first ancient recipe here is for mussels as

they were enjoyed in Rome during the reign

of the very naughty Emperor Tiberius. It is

derived from the work *De re coquinaria* or

Apicius.

Bust of Tiberius Found at Herculaneum

We will never be certain whether that well-heeled first century fellow the gourmet

Marcus Gavius Apicius wrote the work, even

though this old fellow seemed to be a most

likely candidate for the eponymous cookbook.

Some claim the mysterious and possibly

apocryphal Caelius 'Knuckles' Apicius penned

the work.

De re coquinaria has survived largely from

two ninth-century manuscripts

In the fifteenth century those naughty

Renaissance folk rediscovered, *De re*

coquinaria as a useful cookbook which also

included all manner of other insights into the

Roman culinary world

In its original translated form the recipe is:

Liber IX, Thalassa

IX. in metulis: liquamen porrum concisum

cuminum passum satureiam, uinum; mixtum

facies aquatius et ibi mitulos quoques.

Book 9, From the sea.

9. Mussels: liquamen, leeks, passum, savory, wine. Dilute the mixture with water, and boil the mussels in it.

Two tasty sauces for the mussels are further included:

VI. in ostreis: piper ligusticum oui uitellum

acetum liquamen oleum et uinum. si uolueris

et mel addes.

6. (Sauce) for oysters: pepper lovage, yolk of egg, vinegar, liquamen, oil and wine. If you wish, add honey.

VII. in omne genus conciliorum: piper ligusticum petroselinum mentam siccam cuminum plusculum mel liquamen. si uoles folium et malabatrum addes.

7.   (Sauce) for all kinds of shellfish: pepper, lovage, parsley, dried mint, lots of cumin, honey, vinegar, liquamen. If you wish, add a bayleef (sic) and folium indicum

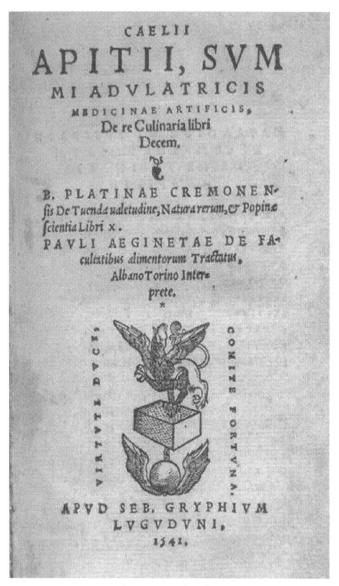

The 1541 Version Including De re Culinaria

A later Edition of Apicius, De Opsoniis et Condimentis (Amsterdam: J. Waesbergios), 1709.

Glossary of these Ancient Ingredients:

Liquamen, or *garum*: a clear 'fishy sauce' liquid made of small fermented fish with salt and sometimes also several kinds of dried herbs.

{You can get an excellent substitute from your local Asian grocery store with either Vietnamese *nuoc-nam*, or Thai *nam-pla*.}

Lovage, *Levisticum officinale*. An umbelliferous plant (like wild celery and parsley) popular in the Ancient Roman kitchen, and still remained very popular in the kitchens of the naughty Middle Ages

Folium Indicum, an Aromatic leaf of a variety of cinnamon tree, *Cinnamomum tamala*. Likely available from your local Indian grocery store. A common ingredient in two of the author's favorites Indian dishes *pillau* and *biryani.*

Passum, a sweet white wine made from partly dried grapes (having a higher sugar content). The old Italian favorite *Santo* Vino Santo or 'holy wine' is traditional in naughty Tuscany. Often considered a dessert wine. The wines may also be described as straw wines since they are often produced by drying the freshly freshly picked naughty grapes on straw mats in a warm and well ventilated area of the house.

A more modern version of the Apicius' Roman classic is found in Ancient Roman Recipes via the excellent food scholarship of Carla Raimer. It is shamelessly set out by the author in all of its glory below:

Ingredients

40-50 mussels

2 tablespoons garum fish sauce

1/2 cup wine

1/2 cup passum (a modern version of this raisin wine is the Italian dessert wine Vin

Santo — see *ante.*)

1 naughty plump well- cleaned leek, well chopped

1 handful of fresh cumin and savory, minced

Method

Wash the mussels thoroughly to remove the sand, then boil them in sufficient water to cover, along with the remaining ingredients.

Serve and enjoy!

2. Aunty Rotter's Mussels Delight

Edna 'Slasher' Rotter was a local village idiot and noted resident of the delightful Suffolk, England village of Woollard End. She kept several goats and climbed trees even into her

90s. She held the county record for field hockey slashings. She was likely as mad as a cut snake but loved muscles and mussels.

Edna 'Slasher' Rotter (tallest back row middle) and Hockey Playing Chums of the ever Dangerous St. Monica's Bruisers (1925)

Ingredients

3/4 pint of fish stock

Kosher or nun-blessed salt and ground

white pepper to taste

1 tb favorite white wine vinegar

4 tablespoon of double cream

3 lbs. fresh well-scrubbed plump naughty

mussels

2 tb cheap dry white wine

1 small yellow onion finely chopped

8 oz leeks very well cleaned and thinly

sliced

2 tablespoons of extra virgin or very

slightly naughty olive oil

1 1/2 oz almonds; ground

2 teaspoons ginger;

a very little piece of naughty saffron

Method

Thoroughly wash and scrub the mussels, scraping off any barnacles, republicans, or French persons.

Remove the beards (unlike Alice Babette Toklas and her pals) and discard any mussels that do not close when given a good tap.

{Very important — if in any doubt discard it!}

Place in a large pan and add a nice splash of the wine.

Cover and cook over a high heat for 5

minutes, shaking the pan until the mussels

have opened. They may squeal with pleasure.

Strain the liquor through a colander into a

bowl and reserve

Heat the oil in a saucepan and soften the

leeks and onions in it for about 3 minutes or

until they are slightly flaccid.

Add the remaining wine and let it reduce by

half.

Stir in the ground almonds and spices.

Mix the reserved cooking liquor with the fish

stock and gradually add it to the pan,

stirring well with a wooden spoon.

Drink two beers or lightly flog a manservant

Leave to simmer gently for 30 minutes or so.

Liquidize the soup and strain through a sieve

into a nice clean saucepan.

Season as necessary, and add a little drizzle

of the wine vinegar.

Discard one half of each mussel shell.

Wave them goodbye as you drink another

nice cold beer

Reheat the soup and stir in the cream and

mussels.

3. Naughty Hamish McSporran's Medieval Mussel and Leek Broth

Semi-professional and quite bonkers Scottish person Hamish Mc. Sporran stumbled around the highlands wearing an attractive kilt and no underwear. It is often claimed that his tottering through a particularly prickly thistle patch awash with local whiskey caused him to both invent Highland Dancing and severely scratch his willy. Mc. Sporran lived in a very lowly croft with his extraordinarily plump wife Betty and their numerous small, sticky spawn. There was always a great mess of mussels available. He was not known a Highland Games caber tosser, just a plain old tosser. However, he

Keith Pepperell with Lady Estima Davenport

kept a nicely hewn caber hidden under the

lowly dwelling just in case.

Since there was no toilet in the croft, the

leeks grown in the ill-kept garden there

were quite spectacular.

Ingredients

3 cups of lobster stock

1/3 cup dry white wine

1/4 teaspoon black pepper

2 pounds mussels

1/2 cup chopped seeded tomato

1 1/2 teaspoons chopped fresh chives

Method

Simmer first 6 ingredients in a stolen Dutch oven over high heat. Add mussels; cover, reduce heat, and cook 4 minutes or until shells open. Remove from heat; discard any unopened shells. Divide mussels and broth evenly between 2 shallow bowls. Sprinkle with tomato and chives.

The Lowly Mc. Sporran Residence

4. Bampdon the Churl's Mussels with Leeks and Local Cider (Scrumpy)

Of all the local beverages that might get a person into trouble scrumpy was certainly the most apt since it had an alcohol content of 79.4%.

Perhaps the best known scrumpy had always been brewed in the South West but the good people of Woollard End in Suffolk had kept their special brand of this crisp apple cider a closely guarded secret. This had been since at least May of 1381 when a local churl called

Piers the Cooper produced the first cask.

The brewing of Pier's extraordinary cider coincided with an attempt by an angry and churlish agent of the Crown, a fellow called Bampton, to collect a three groat poll tax from the frugal locals. Several of these thrifty yeomen attempted to placate and distract poor old churl Bampton with a flagon or two of Pier's the Cooper's scrumpy.

So successful was the attempt that a poor sozzled Bampton stumbled over Suffolk and the delightful neighboring county of Essex for several days thereafter. He shouted out loudly that King Richard II was a bastard and should stick his four groats up his bottom. This of course resulted in the Peasants' Revolt.

Ingredients

one and a half pounds of naughty, fresh and plump mussels

25g best butter

6 ounces of streaky back smoked bacon cut into small bits

2 naughty very well-cleaned small leaks

a quarter cup of fresh thyme (stems

removed)

glass of local cider (blinding scrumpy is best!)

Method

Scrub and de-beard the mussels. Heat half the butter in a pan, then sizzle the bacon for away for 3-4 mins until starting to brown. Make sure not to set the croft on fire or burn the bacon. Add the naughty leeks and the de-stemmed thyme, then sweat everything together for 4-5 mins until soft and nicely flaccid. Turn the heat up high, add the mussels and cider (scrumpy is best) then cover and cook for 4-5 mins, shaking the pan occasionally, until the mussels have opened. Discard any that don't open. Make sure you don't let any bad ones slip by – they must always open! Scoop the mussels and the other naughty bits into a dish, then place the pan back on the heat.

Boil in the lovely moist juices for 1 min or so with the rest of the butter, then pour over the mussels and serve with a loaf of stolen crusty bread and a bucket of blindingly alcoholic scrumpy.

On no account attempt to plough a field or operate a windmill.

A Happy Simpleton- Bampton the Churl

5. Colonel Sir William Pepperell's Moules Marinières (Seafaring Man's Mussels)

Sir William Pepperell with a Favorite Rolling Pin Just Prior to Thrashing the French

My cousin Sir William Pepperell's favorite, and somewhat ironic, celebratory dish *Moules Marinières* was made by Lady Pepperell's well-flogged kitchen staff with fresh, inexpensive ingredients. The traditional version is from naughty Normandy and is made with froggy cider but Sir William preferred to use dry white wine.

Sir William Pepperell from Kittery, Maine, the author's second cousin eight times removed, was a merchant ship-owner, commander of the colonial forces that took Louisbourg, Île Royale (Cape Breton Island), in 1745. He was born on 27 June 1696 at

Kittery Point, Massachusetts (now in Maine),

son of William Pepperell and Margery Bray;

m. 1723 to Mary Hirst, daughter of a

wealthy Boston merchant and

granddaughter of Judge Samuel Sewall, the

diarist; they had four children.

Scribbler Nathaniel Hawthorne wrote of Sir

William in 1833:

"The arms of Great Britain were not

crowned by a more brilliant achievement

during that unprosperous war; and, in

adjusting the terms of a subsequent peace, Louisburg was an equivalent for many losses nearer home. The English, with very pardonable vanity, attributed the conquest chiefly to the valor of the naval force.

On the Continent of Europe, our fathers met with greater justice, and Voltaire has ranked this enterprise of the husbandmen of New England among the most remarkable events in the reign of Louis XV. The ostensible leaders did not fall of reward. Shirley, originally a lawyer, was commissioned in the regular army, and rose to the supreme military command in America. Warren, also,

received honors and professional rank, and

arrogated to himself, without scruple, the

whole crop of laurels gathered at Louisburg.

Pepperell was placed at the head of a royal

regiment, and, first of his countrymen, was

distinguished by the title of baronet.

Vaughan alone, who had been soul of the

deed from its adventurous conception till the

triumphant close, and in every danger and

every hardship had exhibited a rare union of

ardor and perseverance, Vaughan was

entirely neglected, and died in London,

whither he had gone to make known his

claims. After the great era of his life,

Sir William Pepperell did not distinguish

himself either as a warrior or a statesman.

He spent the remainder of his days in all the

pomp of a colonial grandee, and laid down

his aristocratic head among the humbler

ashes of his fathers, just before the

commencement of the earliest troubles

between England and America."

Ingredients

2 tablespoons unsalted best favorite

butter

1 small naughty plump well-cleaned

leek, white and **light** green parts only,

very thinly sliced

1 small shallot nice and thinly sliced

4 medium cloves naughty plump fresh

garlic, thinly sliced

2 bay leaves

Kosheror nun-blessed salt and freshly

ground white pepper

1 cup white wine

2 pounds mussels - well cleaned, no naughty

beards

2 to 3 tablespoons mayonnaise, crème

fraîche, or heavy cream (optional)

1 tablespoon juice and 1 teaspoon grated zest from 1 Mayer lemon

3 tablespoons minced fresh parsley leaves (naughty, annoying stalks removed)

Extra mayonnaise, crème fraîche, or heavy cream for serving

1 loaf of naughty locally baked rustic bread, thickly sliced, drizzled with extra virgin or only slightly naughty olive oil, and broiled until heavily and delightfully toasted (don't burn it).

Directions

Melt 1 tablespoon of the unsalted butter in a saucepan over medium-low heat. Add well-cleaned naughty leeks, shallot, garlic, and bay leaf. Season lightly with kosher or nun-blessed salt and quite heavily with ground white pepper and cook, stirring, until vegetables are very soft and flaccid about 10 minutes or two glasses of wine should do the trick.

Increase heat to high and add the wine. Secretly drink the rest of the bottle when nobody is looking and claim it all went into the dish. Bring to a nice rolling boil and let reduce by about half. A couple of minutes at least should do nicely . Add the well-cleaned naughty mussels (no naughty beards), stir, cover, and cook, shaking pan constantly and peeking every 30 seconds to stir. As soon as **all** the mussels are open (make sure you discard any **non-opened** rascals, transfer mussels to a bowl using tongs (otherwise they could burn your pinkies). Cover to keep mussels all snugly and warm.

Remove from heat and gently whisk in the remaining butter along with mayonnaise or crème fraîche. Return mussels to pot, add parsley (with annoying stalks removed),

Mayer lemon juice, and Mayer lemon zest,

stir to combine, then transfer to a warm

attractive serving bowl. Serve immediately

with additional mayonnaise (if using) and

broiled bread. Toast the naughty French

while you gobble with several bottles of wine.

The Pepperell House in Kittery Point, Maine

6. Lady Joan Pepperell's Naughty Baked Nedging, Suffolk Mussels

Lady Cumberland only made certain dishes

to take to The Ladies Auxiliary Meetings in the Village Hall. She found some dishes "the foul chow of the less than fully civilized". Green bean casseroles and the vile barbecued chip-chop ham were notable among them Her baked bean recipe for example produced almost immediate raucous, hot, searing wind to her Ladyship's considerable delight. The meetings in the Village Hall were invariably very brief indeed. Miss Edna Stallybrass' wind was particularly loud and resonated unpleasantly around the Village Hall like a well struck squash ball.

Her Ladyship was fond of mussels and obtained the recipe from a vulgar American serviceman Lt. Col. Buzz 'Stinky' Quimby whom she meet in a bunker during an air raid over London in WW II during which atrocity she served in the Royal Airforce. Stinky had wandering hands and was "as intelligent as a biscuit" her ladyship recalled.

Ingredients

Naughty mussels – 2 pounds fresh and well-cleaned – no beards!

Half ounce fresh de-stemmed curly parsley – well chopped

1 fat naughty garlic clove - well chopped

Small chili de-seeded and chopped quite finely

6 ounces of breadcrumbs

A goodly cup of freshly grated Parmesan cheese

75m of extra virgin or slightly naughty olive oil

Kosher or nun-blessed salt and ground white pepper to season

Method

Heat your the oven to 200°C /180°C fan, or gas mark 6.

Scrub the naughty mussels well with a small metal brush and wash under running water. Then, bring to a boil over high heat.

Cook until the mussels open (discard any that do not open). Drain (keep 1 cup of the cooking water and drain to remove any nasty looking impurities)

Remove the empty halves of the shells and discard (they may be used for camping see ante) and place the halves containing the mussels on a nice large clean baking tray.

Wash the parsley, remove the annoying stalks, shake dry, and chop finely.

Heat about 45 ml of extra-virgin olive oil in a non-stick pan and fry the breadcrumbs, stirring, until golden brown. Throw away and start again in you burn them. Drink a nice cold beer. Mix together the parsley, chilli, breadcrumbs, Parmesan cheese, garlic, 30 ml of extra-virgin olive oil and the mussel water until you have a delightfully moist mixture that holds together. Season with kosher or nun-blessed salt and ground white peppers.

Place a little of the mixture on top of each baked mussel and press down ever so slightly. Put the baking tray into the preheated oven for about 2 minutes, until the gratin topping is nicely browned. Serve the naughty mussels all lovely and hot and bothered with a lot of white wine. Avoid overly popular Chardonnay if you can!

Lady Joan Enjoying a Moistener at her Local
Pub The Pig and Whistle

7. Lady Ophelia Merkin's Mussolini Mussels

Lady Merkin, elder daughter of noted rake

and Shavian scholar Quimbus Merkin DD,

MC, met bull-chested Mussolini at a social

event when she was Cultural Attache to the

British Embassy in 1925, two years after he

had become Prime Minister of Italy (at the

invitation of noted cross-dresser King Victor Emmanuel III).

She recalled he had been editor of the newspaper *Il Popolo d'Italia* and had written some excellent recipes in his column *Cook Today, Il Duce Tomorrow*. Lady Ophelia referred to him as 'a rum looking cove with shifty eyes and troubled **by hot seering wind'**. He wrote the recipe down on a napkin and gave it to Lady Merkin.

Ingredients

1 (12 ounce) package fettuccine pasta

1 tablespoon olive oil

Keith Pepperell with Lady Estima Davenport

1 onion, chopped

2 cloves garlic, minced

1 (16 ounce) can diced tomatoes

1 teaspoon tomato paste

5 fresh mushrooms, chopped

1 teaspoon dried basil

1/2 teaspoon dried oregano

1 teaspoon dried tarragon

36 raw green-lipped mussels

1/2 cup olives (optional)

2 fresh tomatoes, chopped

Directions

Bring a large pot of water to a nice rolling

boil. Cook pasta in boiling water until well over al dente (al dente is for people with teeth not the English, babies, or the elderly, about 12 minutes. Drain. Meanwhile, heat extra virgin or slightly naughty olive oil in a large pan over medium heat. Cook onion and garlic in the oil until all soft, translucent and flaccid. Take care not to burn.

Stir in the diced tomatoes, tomato paste, and mushrooms, and add the naughty mussels.

Season with the basil, oregano, and tarragon. Cover, and simmer for 10-12 minutes.

Stir in the naughty olives and fresh

tomatoes.

Cover, and simmer for a further 5 minutes.

Serve mussels and sauce over the naughty pasta.

Try not to invade Abyssinia.

Plump Benito Mussolini Reading his
Mussel Recipe to a Group of Fascist Foodies

8. Amitrasudan 'Ernie' Bhagwat's Curried Mussels

Naughty Amitrasudan Bhagwat, whose

Indian first name translated as 'destroyer of

enemies', was a genial shiny brown fellow

who had arrived at the delightful Suffolk, England village of Sandon Bottom as a small boy concealed by his anxious parents in the luggage of noted local good old boy Bunty Frobisher'.

This was accomplished just before Bunty's return from 'doing something' for the Raj in Bombay. Bunty lived in the newly converted old stable block at the impressive county pile that was Woodruffe Hall.

The Bhagwat's had provided ample food and drink for their shiny brown boy who came to learn English through the air holes bored through Bunty Frobisher's largest suitcase

during the fifty-eight day sea voyage.

Unfortunately, the ripeness of the expletives

of the various foul-mouthed seafaring men,

who couldn't work out just where the small

cans of ablutions in the luggage hold were

coming from, provided little Amitrasudan

with the vocabulary of a Spittlefield Market

meat cutter.

The Bhagwat's had always dreamed of a

career in news agency for their little

destroyer of enemies and as it transpired he

was not not going to let them down.

Old Bunty Frobisher himself found the little

tike fast asleep in his largest suitcase

together with some polo mallets when he

was supervising unpacking at Woodruffe Hall.

The little fellow soon awoke and greeted

Frobisher's faithful old manservant Quizzling

with a shrill "How's your cock mate?'

Years later, when old Basil 'Punchy Fudge

who had been the news agent in Woollard

End for over fifty years finally gave up the

ghost, Ernie took over, with the help of a

little inheritance he had got from The

Frobisher Estate. Ernie had been a star pupil

at Woollard End School of News agency.

Almost immediately Ernie brought his very aged parents over from Bombay and they now resided over his shop. The marvelous aromas of Mrs Indira Bhagwat's goat saagwala and aloo tikki with chola wafted invitingly down Kipling Avenue bringing back to dear old Blighty fond memories for the several old buffers and their memsahibs who had spent time blundering around in The Raj.

Once, at the annual Woollard End Talent Contest in The Rudyard Kipling Village Hall, Bhagwat had honored the village with an appearance as Tennessee 'Ernie' Bhagwat wearing unnecessarily tight leather trousers and accompanying himself on an electric sitar. His rendition of Peggy Singh brought the house down, and most particularly when he had thrown immaculately laudered handkerchiefs courtesy of Mrs. Nana Poonani's Wishy Washy Laundry to the ladies rapturously moistening in the front row. One had actually exclaimed quite loudly that she had always assumed that circumcision was universal in the Indian sub-continent. Oddly too, Ernie was probably the only Indian never to have played cricket.

His curried mussels were a considerable local favorite.

Ingredients

8 plump naughty shallots, minced

6 cloves garlic, minced

12 fl oz cheap dry white wine

1 pot double cream

1 teaspoon Madras curry powder

32 mussels – cleaned and debearded

1 oz best butter

A handful of clean minced parsley (with annoying stems removed)

A goodly handful well-chopped spring onions

Method

In a large pan, cook the naughty shallots and garlic in simmering and bubbling away wine until all flaccid and nicely translucent.

Stir in the cream and Madras curry powder. When the sauce is heated through and very gently bubbling away immediately add the naughty mussels. Cover, and then steam mussels for a few minutes, until their shells open wide. With a slotted spoon, transfer steamed mussels to a bowl, leaving the sauce in the pan. **Discard any unopened mussels.**

Whisk the butter into the cream sauce. Turn off the heat, and stir in parsley and spring onions.

Serve immediately with several bottles of ice cold Indian beer. Try not to flog the help.

Major Bunty Frobisher Having his Toenails Varnished by His Manservant Mr. Gupta in Readiness for A Dance at the British Club

9. Naughty Mr. Han's Vietnamese Coconut Curry Mussels

Mr. Han is a delightful fellow and an occasional drinking companion of the author

Han is an exceptionally good chef and the author has been honored to sample many of his dishes. This naughty recipe is a slight variation of Mr. Han's original preparation. Lemongrass can be purchased ready prepared if desired but Mr. Han insists it is not quite as good.

Ingredients
2 stalks fresh lemon grass

4 tablespoons favorite vegetable oil

2 medium red plump fresh onions, thinly sliced

6 cloves garlic, thinly sliced

6 tablespoons chopped and peeled fresh ginger

1/4 cup green curry paste

2 15-ounce cans coconut milk

4 tablespoons Vietnamese fish sauce (see ante)

6 pounds fresh plump naughty mussels, scrubbed and debearded

4 nice fresh limes, halved

1 cup chopped fresh cilantro (stems

removed)

Method

Trim the lemon grass, leaving about 6 inches at the root end; discard the tops. Smash the stalks violently with the flat side of a sturdy knife and cut into 1-inch pieces.

Heat 2 tablespoons vegetable oil in each of 2 large pans over medium-high heat. Add 1 sliced onion to each and cook, stirring, until all naughtily soft, translucent and flaccid, about 5 minutes should do the trick. Add half each of the garlic, lemongrass, ginger and curry paste to each pan and cook, stirring with a wooden spoon, until nice and golden, about 2 minutes. Drink two beers.

Add 1 can coconut milk, 2 tablespoons fish sauce and 1/4 cup water to each pan and bring to a gentle naughty simmer. Divide the mussels between the pans; cover and cook, stirring occasionally, until the mussels open, about 8 minutes should suffice. (**Discard any that do not open**.) Add the juice of 2 limes to each pan, then add the lime halves. Stir 1/2 cup cilantro into each. Serve with bread and lots of nice ice cold beer.

Mr. Han Sitting Pensively on a Large Rock
Hoping to Spot a Rare Breed of Vole

10. Adrian Garsed's Naughty Spanish Mussels

The author's long time chum, drinking

companion, and cricket team member Mr.

Garsed was at Leeds University in the 1960s

with the author. His family farmed in

Oxfordshire. His most excellent Clos Garsed

(1989) was an exceptional vintage. Adrian

continues to reside in gentile semi-

retirement in the Priorat region of Spain.

Ingredients

6 ounces of Mussels

4 ounces of naughty carrots

6 ounces of Tomatoes

1 green peppers

Sherry vinegar

Coriander leaves

3 tablespoon Olive oil

1 pinch kosher or nun-blessed salt

1 pinch ground white pepper

Method

Cook the peeled, washed and sliced carrots with a little bit of water and olive oil in a skillet for 15 minutes.

Clean and scrape the mussels. Put them in a pot, and cook until they open. Discard any naughty unopened ones. Reserve the cooked mussels by letting them cool and put them on an attractive brightly colored plate, each in half of the shell.

Peel the tomatoes, dice them thinly. Empty the pepper of seeds and inner white bits and dice it up.

Mix the vegetables with the oil and the

vinegar, add some kosher or nun-blessed salt and ground white pepper. Cover each naughty plump mussel with this mixture.

Serve the Spanish mussels with the fried carrots sprinkled over them with the coriander and a nice rare bottle of very fine Clos Garsed wine.

A Naughty Dish of Spanish Mussels

Mejillones escabechados from Spain

11. Lady Estima Davenport's Naughty Chili Tomato Mussels

An English newspaper article reported in 1928, "The Senior Gentlewoman's Invitation Doubles Championships at Wimbledon or the All England Lawn Tennis and Croquet Club was first held in 1877 when Englishwomen the stout Miss Tippy Tollboothe-Change and Miss Honoria Cummerbund prevailed over the ever-plucky French pairing of Miss Humidelèvres and Miss Envracvulve. No English pair had been victorious since.

Lady Estima Davenport and her old school chum and special friend Muriel Dinwiddy had not played at the All England Club in a tournament, although they had taken part in several exhibition games there. The Senior Ladies invitation was a round-robin event of six teams.

It was expected that the valient ladies would meet the hirsuit French pair in the deciding match and as it turned the pundits had predicted wisely.

Both teams had beaten the muscular Dutch pairing of Mrs. Tieten Van Der Tepels en Miss Snavel Klootwijk, the German team of Mrs. Behaard Verbrand und Miss Hinken Hahn and the ever popular Swedish pairing of Miss Stygg Nipplar och Mrs. Enorma Skinka-Vind.

The French pair, the sisters Salomé and Capucine-Enola La Touche (no relation to ex-Nazi Helmut 'La Touche' Funkbrunner), were considered slight favorites at 5-6 over Davenport and Dinwiddy The frogs had just recently won the Spanish Open beating Mrs.

Teta Acaricia and Mrs. Caido Escroto 6-0,

6-1 in only fifty-six minutes.

We are delighted to report that Dinwiddy

and Davenport prevailed in a thrilling match

6-1 6-2. Miss Dinwiddy was, as always

devastating at the net and Lady Davenport's

powerful backhand was a joy to behold."

Ingredients

4 pounds fresh scrubbed de-bearded
mussels

1/4 cup dry white wine or cider

Mayer lemon

8

fresh parsley de-stemmed

For the Chili Tomato Sauce

One pound ripe skinned Roma tomatoes

15 g best butter

2 tablespoons extra virgin or slightly naught olive oil

1 teaspoon smoked paprika

2 teaspoons chopped fresh de-stemmed basil

Kosher or nun-blessed salt and ground white pepper

2 tablespoons tomato paste

1 large white or yellow onion well diced

2 finely chopped cloves of plump naughty garlic

Method for the Naughty sauce

Chop the nice plump ripe Roma tomatoes.

Heat the best butter and olive oil in a pan and fry the diced onions, chopped garlic and chillies until the onion is all flaccid and transparent, taking care not to let them burn

Add the paprika, basil and tomato paste and stir in well with a wooden spoon.

Add a little dry white wine or cider may to loosen the sauce and then add the tomatoes, with a small pinch of sugar.

Simmer for 40 minutes or so and then season with kosher or nun-blessed salt and ground white pepper.

Clean the naughty plump mussels well and debeard them

Place the mussels and dry white wine or cider in a pot over a high heat. Drink some wine or cider.

Cover with a firm lid to steam them

Once they are fully open, strain all the liquid from the pot.

As always discard all that are unopened.

Add the chilli-tomato sauce to the mussels and stir gently to naughtily and sensuously coat all the mussels with the sauce.

Squeeze over half a nice Mayer lemon and garnish the dish with quartered lemons and well chopped de-stemmed parsley.

Serve immediately, with lots of French bread to soak up the naughty juices. Drink a lot of wine or cider. Don't drive or play tennis.

Powerful Lady Estima Davenport Showing a
Fine Backhand at Wimbledon in 1928

ABOUT THE AUTHOR

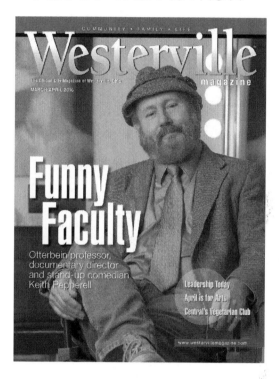

The author is a happy, plump simpleton who has been a TV historian on History and American Heroes Channels, produced and directed award winning documentaries, and written 114 dull books. He is presently a college professor in witness protection somewhere in the mid-west's green bean casserole belt. He is as mad as a cut snake.

Printed in Great Britain
by Amazon